Quantitative Hitting

Surprising Discoveries of
the Game's Best Hitters

The Next *Big Thing*
in Baseball

D.K. Willardson

Copyright © 2018 Hitting Tech, Inc.

All rights reserved. No part of this publication may be reproduced, distributed, or transmitted in any form or by any means, including photocopying, recording, or other electronic or mechanical methods, without the prior written permission of the publisher, except in the case of brief quotations embodied in critical reviews and certain other non-commercial uses permitted by copyright law. For permission requests, write to the publisher, addressed "Attention: Permissions Coordinator," at info@hittingtech.com

Print ISBN: 9781983358487

Contents

Preface 5

Introduction. 7

Chapter 1. Backspin vs. Square Hitting 15

Chapter 2. The Importance of Vertical Bat Angle 25

Chapter 3. Horizontal Bat Angle 33

Chapter 4. Swing Path – It's Not What You Think! . . .39

Chapter 5. Quantifying Optimal Swing Paths 51

Chapter 6. Putting It All Together: The Swing Path and Angles That Make Joey Votto Different 59

Chapter 7. Implementation and Training Methods . . .63

Chapter 8. A Story of Unlikely Discovery 71

Chapter 9. Key Bat and Body Adjustments. 79

Chapter 10. Final Thoughts 83

Endnotes. 89

Glossary 91

Preface

It was never part of my plan to write a book. The discoveries which challenge conventional views on hitting had far greater value through other strategies. I believe the closing of those opportunities, guiding my work in this direction happened for a reason – so that the full credit and glory could go to the source providing the divine inspiration. With the benefit of hindsight, I realize that the findings resulted from the combination of several unlikely sources, each being a critical link in the chain of discovery – all very far from baseball. At the core was a fascination with complex sports motions, combined with a deep interest in discovering opportunity through research.

The focus of the book is the connection between data and hitting mechanics. Initially, the majority of the research was based on analyzing video. In 2015, however, a significant amount of data was made available to the public from major league games through Baseball Savant. The ability to quantify specific mechanics of the game's best hitters changed everything. While video is a great tool, viewers tend to see very different things from the same video based on what they believe to be true. The connection between data and mechanics is something that is being viewed skeptically by both sides of baseball – the analytical side focused on the data has steered clear of mechanics, while the "traditional" coaching and player development side has steered clear of the data. The result is fertile and untrodden turf in the middle of the two polarized camps. From my experience in investment research, one thing is certain – opportunities tend to lurk where they are not believed to exist. It hasn't been the rejection of the ideas per se that has led me to this conclusion, but rather the unwillingness to even consider their existence. The research methodology I used for many years in investment research played a critical role – determine the primary drivers of performance, go deep on those drivers, and continually ask yourself where you might be wrong or what you could be missing.

I believe that the data presented will challenge your views on hitting in some way. I realize, however, that views don't always change based on facts and data. Opinions on hitting tend to run strong, and I certainly don't take for granted that the data will change your views. You will find that most of the research in the book is original work; therefore, few source citations. However, to me, it would be the most egregious form of plagiarism to not give credit and glory to God - for all of it.

Introduction

I believe you will find this book on hitting to be different from any other book you've read on the subject. You will find no philosophies or opinions about hitting – only data-supported discoveries of how a small group of the best hitters in the game are utilizing mechanics different from everyone else. These key mechanical differences are largely independent of talent and can be adopted by players at any level. Regardless of your relationship with baseball, whether you are a player, a coach, an organization, a parent, a researcher, a fantasy baseball enthusiast, or a general baseball fan, there is a competitive advantage to be enjoyed through these findings.

The total number of people in the constituent groups above is significant. Players in the United States alone are estimated at 14.7 million and another 11 million play fantasy baseball.[1] The data and findings suggest that few, if any, of all the participants in the groups above are consciously thinking about swing path *completely* correct as fundamental elements required for a complete and correct understanding have never before been linked to swing path effectiveness. While there appears to be subconscious "knowledge" among a small number of professional hitters, the data, in a way, allows us to extract, quantify, and transfer this knowledge to any of the constituents above who are open to objectively consider the findings.

The title *Quantitative Hitting* may seem intimidating; however, the core principle is very simple – to have a factual basis for accepting or rejecting a particular view regarding hitting mechanics. All the findings that follow can be understood on an intuitive level. The illustrations alone should be sufficient to understand what the data reveals. The chapters are structured with an increasing level of detail and data so that readers can skip to the next chapter at the desired point without missing critical information on each topic.

For each topic or finding, there are two different levels of presentation and discussion – a fact-based case on what the data proves, and then key takeaways from what the data suggests. I point this out so that different views in the second area don't detract from what is factually observable. In a few sections, there is additional discussion of "why" that is included simply because I found it interesting to consider.

The majority of the findings relate directly or indirectly to swing path, which is a major factor in player performance. What follows is a deep dive on the subject, which will examine the actual X, Y, and Z positions that define swing path in a level of detail which has not, to date, been conducted publicly. Importantly, player outperformance and underperformance can be observed through consistent differences in each of the X, Y, and Z positions, suggesting the possibility for a "systematic approach" to completely eliminating swing path as a major cause of underperformance.

A few of the illustrations may require a little work on your part in order to visualize some of the key three-dimensional mechanical findings in a two-dimensional format. There is bat loft on each of the three axes mentioned above that need to be understood to fully appreciate the "true" swing path. Interestingly, most of the findings seem to relate to one another. I believe there is an important story being told by the data regarding superior mechanics. A story which has not been told that challenges conventional views.

Consider the general concept of competitive advantage and opportunity. Whether in managing a company, investing, baseball, or almost any endeavor where consensus views exist, if a participant's view is largely similar to that of the consensus, then there is little opportunity for a competitive advantage. Thus, an advantage exists only if a view is either contrary to the consensus or if it is a view where consensus opinions have not yet been established. Of course, the validity of a view is also a key ingredient and largely goes without saying. The data suggests the findings meet both of these criteria.

For whatever reason, many people in baseball tend to have a high level of attachment to their opinions about hitting. I point this out since there will be significant data presented which challenges existing views on mechanics. On a scale of one to ten, how strongly would you rate your opinions on hitting mechanics? Whether you are at the upper end of the range in terms of attachment to opinions would be good to know when considering data that likely supports a different view. You will get the most value from this book if you are able to check your opinions here, before diving into the contents. One of the reasons I was able to make the discoveries you are about to learn is because I was able to start with a "clean slate", without preconceived opinions. Psychological researchers have identified what is called "confirmation bias", the direct influence of desire on beliefs. In other words, when a person would like a certain idea or concept to be true, they end up believing it to be true, making it difficult to change the original view.

All sports go through transitions where the best players change mechanics for the better. It is almost always the case that the top performers in a particular sport will be well out in front of conventional views. When it comes to baseball, this does not necessarily mean that these hitters who are out in front with more effective mechanics understand in terms of conscious "knowledge" these specific mechanical differences. While a few may, others likely arrived at their current mechanics through an iterative process of continually keeping what works and discarding what doesn't. Regardless of the mix between conscious and subconscious mechanics, we can be relatively sure that consensus views, just by the nature of how they are formed, will generally lag positive mechanical trends.

Let's start by taking a look at a metric that can be measured or estimated with reasonable accuracy yet is not part of any public dataset, likely because it is not believed to be important. As shown in the table below, the difference in player performance based on this metric is sizable. Players represent MLB Qualified Hitters from 2015-2017 (inclusive membership for all years required).[2]

Quartile	Batting Average on Balls in Play (BABIP)	Weighted Runs Created (wRC+)
I	0.324	129
IV	0.300	105

To put the above metric in perspective, consider that it outperforms the top quartile of high exit velocity hitters who have an average BABIP of .316 and wRC+ of 127. Players in the top quartile whose names you might recognize include Mike Trout, Joey Votto, and Miguel Cabrera. Performance for the fourth quartile is not necessarily "bad" from an absolute perspective; however, relative to the Qualified Hitters (minimum 502 plate appearances required each year), they are significantly underperforming the average BABIP of .308 and WRC+ of 115.

In the next few chapters, you will learn more about this metric as well as the data which suggests the outperformance is being driven significantly by key mechanical differences that could be incorporated by most all players. A metric of significance on par with the all-important exit velocity, yet it has never been publicly examined.

Any guesses about what the metric might be?

The metric is the amount of backspin on hit balls.

Given that, would you guess that the high backspin hitters are in the top or bottom performance quartile?

Yes, of course, backspin has been preached for years as a desirable goal for hitters. Further, the principles of basic physics indicate that a ball hit with backspin will travel farther than a ball hit flat or "square". So case closed – the backspin hitters are the better performers, right?

Actually, the correct answer is the opposite – backspin hitters are in the *under-performing* group! The data indicates the "cost" of a backspin approach is very high and outweighs the benefit of increased distance. We will get into more detail on this and many other areas where consensus views are misplaced or don't exist. At this point, you would be forgiven for believing that talent is driving the outperformance of the square hitting group. What the data shows, however, is that these hitters are utilizing different mechanics, that are likely independent of talent and could be implemented by a hitter at any level.

What makes the new data-driven discoveries in hitting so exciting is that there is a trend currently in progress. Identifying major shifts in any area is considerably easier after-the-fact. As a former professional investor, I believe the opportunity in the findings to be presented exceeds those I observed in the investment profession by a wide margin. Given the large research budgets and staffs across professional baseball, I have spent considerable time thinking about why these opportunities have been missed. Thoughts on this will be discussed in later chapters.

For each finding, there is an opportunity for initial improvement simply by understanding the key mechanical practices and how and why they differ from consensus views. In other words, simply changing a view is "low-hanging fruit" for improvement. Beyond this "easy" improvement is an opportunity for maximizing performance through a well-defined, high-precision training process to transfer the new information into muscle memory where it can be used effectively. Implementation and training methods for both options are covered in an upcoming chapter.

The data and results encourage consideration that systematic identification and improvement are possible as a result of quantifying key mechanical drivers of performance. I believe this challenges current views that a systematic approach to player development and "repair" is not possible. With that said, however, *Quantitative Hitting* is not a one-size-fits-all approach and can be tailored for player individuality *within* a systematic process. My hope is that you will not only benefit from the contents of the book but that it might also provide a framework for considering the effectiveness of discoveries in the future. I sincerely thank you for your purchase and wish you success regardless of your role in the sport.

Chapter 1.
Backspin vs. Square Hitting

It is easy to understand why many believe that backspin is a potential performance improvement strategy. After all, balls hit with high amounts of backspin travel farther and achieve high levels of performance. *Wait, so you are telling me that balls hit with high levels of backspin outperform but the players who hit those balls perform well below average?*

Yes, that is exactly what the data shows. The table below shows the BABIP performance of well-hit-fly-balls based on backspin quartile.

Spin Impact (ft) Quartiles	# Of Players	Single	Double	Triple	HR	Outs	BABIP
<-10.2	806	1,965	3,390	255	1,200	605	0.335
>-10.2 to 2.3	842	582	2,653	349	2,765	11,024	0.236
>2.3 to 14.0	838	415	2,943	424	4,390	9,291	0.279
>14.0	861	380	3,374	563	7,614	5,722	0.417

The balls in the highest spin category perform the best, followed by the lowest spin category. Notice the smaller number of players hitting the lowest spin balls. This suggests the low-spin, square hitters are earning the most at bats as a result of better performance (note the number of balls hit is the same in each quartile). The chart below makes it quite clear that the "cost" of hitting with high backspin is considerably greater than the benefit as the square hitters significantly outperform.

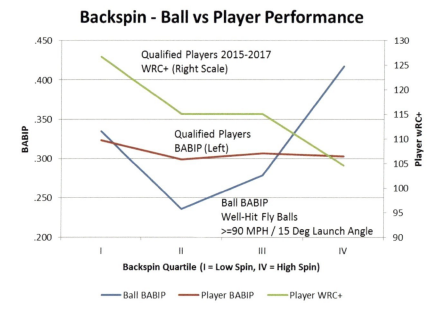

The classification of spin groups for both balls and players is based on well-hit balls with exit velocities greater than 90 MPH and launch angles between 15 and 45 degrees. Given the information from the prior two charts, the importance of ball-versus-player results cannot be overstated. Players cannot hit only the "good backspin" balls as they also must accept the "bad" outcomes associated with that

Chapter 1. Backspin vs. Square Hitting

approach. Thus, in considering the data, a player's options are limited to "all-in" player outcomes, which include a *distribution of results*. This ball-versus-player outcome difference also comes into play in choosing launch angle goals, which will be discussed later.

Correlation Analysis - Not Always the Best Tool

In considering the relationship between spin and performance, a typical correlation chart would be generated for analysis.

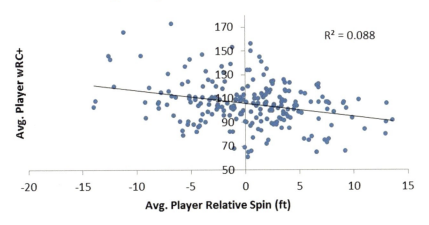

Generally, the R^2 would be evaluated for connection to performance. In this case, relative backspin explains 8.8% of the variation in performance, which is not very high. The key takeaway from the above chart, however, is that *none* of the extremely high performing players (wRC+ > 135) are utilizing a high backspin approach. Likewise, *none* of the very poor performing players (wRC+ <80) are hitting the ball with extremely low levels of backspin. Thus, in looking for early indicators of what the best hitters might be doing differently, the outliers, rather than the R^2, may provide more valuable information, as illustrated below.

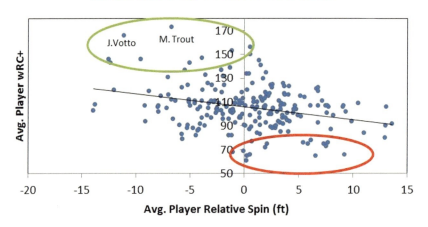

In looking at the exit velocity (EV), launch angle (LA), and distance, the impact of spin is evident:

	Square Hitters	Backspin Hitters	Difference
Avg. Exit Velocity - Well Hit Balls	99.4	98.7	0.7
Avg. Launch Angle - Well Hit Balls	21.5	18.5	3.0
Avg. Distance - Well Hit Balls	339.6	347.6	-8.0
Spin Impact (ft)	-7.7	5.7	-13.4

The square hitters had a .7 MPH exit velocity advantage and a 3° loft advantage relative to the high backspin group which combined, would typically result in approximately 20 feet of additional distance. However, the distance for the

Chapter 1. Backspin vs. Square Hitting

square hitting group was actually eight feet *less* than that of the backspin hitting group. With respect to the potential randomness of players and spin, the data indicates "stickiness" to the spin groups as only one player switched from the high spin to the low spin group (or vice versa) over the 2015-2017 seasons.

Details related to the specific swing path differences of the two groups will be discussed shortly. The results of these mechanical differences are higher infield fly balls (IFFB%), greater volatility of launch angles (as measured by standard deviation), and a higher propensity to pull middle-middle pitches as illustrated below:

	Square Hitters	Backspin Hitters	Difference
Infield Fly Ball Rate (IFFB%)	4.6	11.2	-6.6
Standard Deviation of Launch Angle	23.3	25.7	-2.4
Horizontal Angle	2.5	6.8	-4.3

Intuitively, the higher IFFB rate for the high backspin hitting group is not too difficult to understand given the lower ball contact point (relative to the ball equator) for both backspin and IFFBs. This will be made clear with some illustrations in the next chapter. Possibly the strongest case for meaningfully different paths and bat angles between the groups is a breakdown of loft by pitch location. Notice how the square hitters are showing much more loft on all pitch locations as well as more loft consistency horizontally across the strike zone

	Square Hitters	Backspin Hitters	Difference
Average Lanch Angle - Inside	18.0	12.3	5.7
Average Launch Angle - Middle	16.9	11.0	5.9
Average Launch Angle - Outside	14.9	8.2	6.7

Exit velocity (EV) of hit balls is broadly believed to be one of the most important factors in performance. The data clearly supports this view as players with high EVs tend to outperform those with low EVs. However, in comparing the performance between EV and spin of the top and bottom quartiles of both metrics, spin outperforms EV at the upper levels of plate appearances (PA).

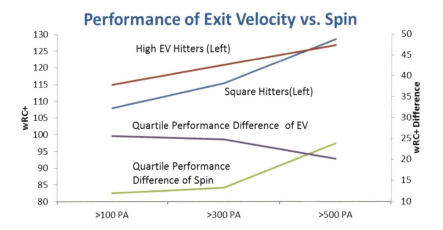

This is really quite remarkable. As plate appearances increase, the "noise" of the short-term outperformance of high backspin balls is essentially extracted, revealing the high value of a square hitting approach. The quartile differences (bottom two lines) suggest meaningful upside for players who can change from a backspin to a square approach.

What the Data Suggests

If swing path is indeed a primary driver of performance, then hitting the ball square (vs. with backspin) appears to be a driver *within a driver*. Notice that by just grouping based on relative spin, several other important elements – low launch angle volatility, low IFFB rate, and significantly improved launch angle profiles – all consistently align. No other metric aligns these other factors in a similar fashion.

A simple experiment can provide insight into why these factors are consistently aligning. Take bat and ball like objects (one-handed swings are recommended) and try to hit the ball with backspin at a certain launch angle – say approximately 20°. Then, in the next round of hits, try to hit the ball flat or square at the same 20° launch angle. What you will likely notice is that the path for the backspin hits actually has less loft than for the square hits (evidenced by inadvertent hits at a very low launch angle). You will also likely notice fewer pop-ups, lower launch angle variability, and higher overall loft for the square-hit balls.

Since "hit with backspin" has been popular for some time, the data suggests an attractive opportunity for players to improve their results by either eliminating this objective or substituting it with a "square-hit" philosophy. Given the improvement potential based on the data of approximately 23% among the Qualified Hitters from 2015-2017, the opportunity would seem even greater at the lower levels (minor leagues, college, high school, etc.).

An interesting observation in the data is the relationship

between player size and the level of backspin employed. The players in the square hitting group are physically larger than the players in the high backspin group. This relationship is also evident in the larger datasets with lower requirements for minimum plate appearances. Here is the relationship for the Qualified Player dataset:

Spin Quartile I=Low, IV = High	Height (Inches)	Weight	Avg. Distance
I	74.1	217.3	339.6
II	72.8	212.0	343.8
III	73.3	211.8	345.1
IV	72.1	203.4	347.6

One possible explanation for this size-spin connection is that, whether consciously or subconsciously, players learn that hitting with backspin increases distance. Since the larger players generally have more natural power, they haven't needed to use backspin to "keep up" with their peers in terms of distance. The data suggests the smaller players may be blinded to the "cost" side of the equation and are focused more on the extra distance. It could also be a selection issue where distance is incorrectly viewed as "power", causing those players to be promoted through the system. Several potential implications should be considered. Is the typical pre-game batting practice where many players go for home runs causing or contributing to the issue? Ego is a very real issue, and typical batting practice sessions may be unknowingly changing the paths of the smaller hitters to generate more backspin.

Chapter 1. Backspin vs. Square Hitting   23

The Method and Model Used to Estimate Relative Backspin

There is a high-tech TrackMan system at all MLB parks which captures three-axis spin data for both pitched and hit balls; however, only the pitch data is publicly available through Baseball Savant. While the lack of this data in the public domain prevents analysis from an absolute perspective, a relative assessment of these factors can be made by utilizing the publicly available data as follows:

Average distances for well-hit fly balls (≥90 MPH, ≥15°<45°) at each exit velocity and launch angle combination between 90-115 MPH and 15°-45°, respectively, were used to create a model of expected distance. The dataset was for 2015-2016 (excluding all balls hit at Coors Field). The distance difference for each hit was then examined based on the horizontal angle of the hit. The pattern of the distance differences indicates there is a significant directional bias likely caused by spin, as illustrated below. The impact of spin on the flight of the baseball has been studied extensively with a link noted between spin, distance, and ball flight.[3] Separate models were created for right-handed and left-handed hitters. The following illustration is based on right-handed hitters only.

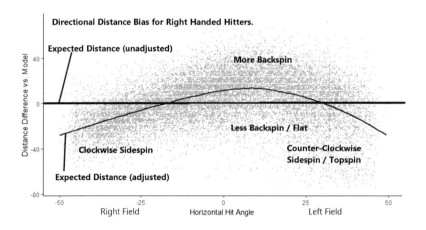

Average, directionally adjusted distance differences were calculated for the qualified player dataset from 2015-2017. In order to reduce the potential impact of park-specific atmospheric conditions, all balls hit at a player's home park were excluded in addition to all balls hit at Coors Field. Average residual values were computed for each player, and the top and bottom quartiles were examined for meaningful differences between the low-backspin and high-backspin hitting groups.

Chapter 2.
The Importance of Vertical Bat Angle

Vertical Bat Angle (VBA) may be the single largest mechanical change in professional baseball over the past several years. Even though VBA has changed considerably, a major link to performance has not been publicly considered. If you've watched baseball games or highlights from the past, you may have noticed that players previously hit with more horizontal bat positions. After all, very reputable sources such as Ted Williams advocated front knee bend as the primary adjustment for low pitches in order to maintain a more horizontal bat position through the swing.[4] This is clearly not the method being employed by the best hitters in the game today. Following are illustrations of Vertical Bat Angle.

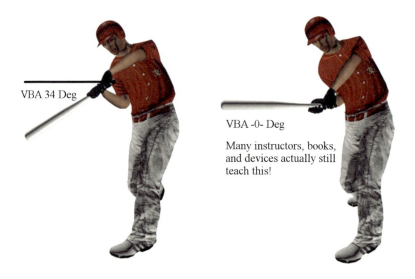

Although the general trend has been towards increased levels of VBA for all pitch locations (and even more so for low and inside pitch locations), there is still considerable divergence among the VBAs of professional baseball. As it turns out, one of the key mechanical differences in the flat hitting group (flat in terms of ball contact, not launch angle) is the use of increased Vertical Bat Angle relative to the backspin hitting group. Given the relationship between high infield fly ball (IFFB) rates and backspin as previously examined, one would expect lower Vertical Bat Angles (i.e., more horizontal bat positions) at contact for those players with high IFFB rates. That is exactly what the data suggests. The following chart is based on the highest and lowest IFFB rates over the 2015-2017 seasons and the hitter's VBA for a middle-middle pitch location as obtained from video samples.

Chapter 2. The Importance of Vertical Bat Angle

Lowest	IFFB%	VBA	Highest	IFFB%	VBA
Joey Votto	0.8%	37	Todd Frazier	18%	23
Joe Mauer	2.3%	31	Jose Bautista	16%	23
Christian Yelich	2.7%	31	Kevin Pillar	16%	32
Miguel Cabrera	3.7%	33	Brian Dozier	16%	24
Matt Carpenter	3.7%	31	Carlos Santana	14%	26
Chris Davis	4.3%	39	Xander Bogaerts	14%	29
Buster Posey	4.9%	36	Manny Machado	14%	22
Kendrys Morales	5.0%	33	Mark Trumbo	14%	28
Mike Trout	5.2%	39	Edwin Encarnacion	13%	32
DJ LeMahieu	5.7%	33	Mookie Betts	13%	27
Average	3.8%	34	Average	15%	27

The players with low IFFB rates, who are also in the top-quartile, low-spin group, are highlighted in blue while the players who are in the bottom quartile (most backspin) are highlighted in red. The overlap, as indicated above, suggests a relationship between the use of backspin and the tendency to hit "pop-ups". The illustration below may help you to visualize the benefits of greater levels of VBA.

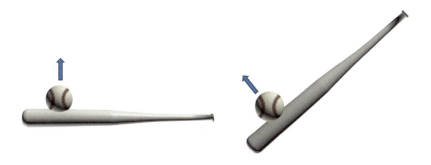

The contact properties shown above are consistent with the data. As VBA increases, the probability of hitting the bottom of the ball decreases, thereby contributing to less backspin, a lower IFFB rate, and lower launch angle variability, all positive effects. In comparing the two contact points, you'll notice the hitter on the right has traded vertical variability for more performance-friendly horizontal variability. Also, in the contact point on the left, the ball has a greater probability of landing in the field of play and being caught for an easy out whereas in the contact position on the right, the ball has a greater probability of being hit foul and out of play.

Vertical Bat Angle also changes with pitch location – more VBA for lower and inside pitches and less for higher and outside pitches. A study of minor league players in 2011 by David Fortenbaugh identified a clear link between pitch location and VBA.[5]

	Vertical Bat Angle		
	Inside	Middle	Outside
High	24	22	21
Middle	32*	30	28*
Low	39	36	33
*Author estimate.			

Note the VBA of 30° for the middle-middle location observed in the study relative to the two groups above. The flat-hitting, low-IFFB group had higher VBAs, while the high-backspin, high-IFFB group had lower VBAs for this pitch location.

Chapter 2. The Importance of Vertical Bat Angle

Outside of historical video, there is no data on VBA over time; however, it is interesting to consider the trend of IFFB rates in professional baseball as shown in the chart below. It is very possible that this trend is related, at least in part, to the trend of increasing VBA levels.

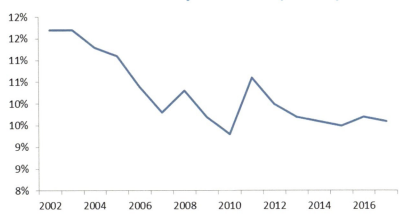

If you have an interest in understanding the magnitude of this change, I highly recommend viewing video of older swings, many of which can be accessed with a simple Internet search. As is evident, even among current players with low levels of VBA, these levels are still considerably higher than those of past players. This trend appears to be in progress, and many players could achieve considerable upside through a better understanding of the benefits of higher levels of VBA.

Greater VBA leads to improved launch angle consistency …

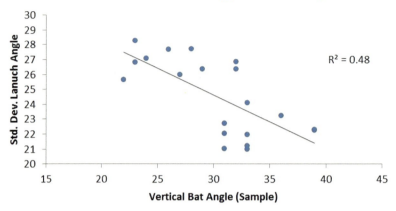

... and improved launch angle consistency leads to better performance.

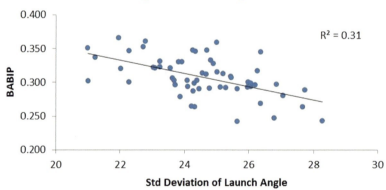

What the Data Suggests

The data on VBA suggests that popular hitting tools such as the common baseball tee are likely discouraging a healthy

Chapter 2. The Importance of Vertical Bat Angle 31

level of VBA. Since higher levels of VBA cause greater contact with the tee stem, more effective training tools should be considered. Training tools and methods will be discussed in a separate chapter. Thus far, the data clearly indicates a link between low backspin, VBA, and performance. For many players, simply eliminating the "backspin" and "flat bat" goals will result in substantial improvement.

Given the connection between VBA and square, low-spin contact, increasing VBA may be the single largest opportunity for general improvement for players at all levels. Examining the amounts of VBA at the various levels of baseball shows that those with more VBA progress further in their baseball careers.

Playing Level	Vertical Bat Angle (VBA)
Professional - Major League	25° to 35°
Professional - Minor League	24° to 34°
College	23° to 33°
High School - Varsity	21° to 31°
High School – Junior Varsity	20° to 30°
Middle School	17° to 27°
Youth	15° to 25°
Source: Blast Motion	

At present, there appear to be two different schools of thought regarding VBA – both of which are misplaced. The "traditional" view maintains that a level swing and the horizontal bat position that accompanies it are important components of a "good" swing. Many training devices have these views imbedded as key objectives. The second and more progressive view of VBA is that players' differing levels of VBA result primarily from their individual style or swing. What is not broadly believed or even known is the relationship of VBA to square, low-spin contact, improved launch angle consistency, and overall performance.

A popular view is that IFFBs, or "pop-ups" result from too much loft in a player's swing path or from "dropping the bat head". The data, however, overwhelmingly supports the likelihood that pop-ups occur for the exact opposite reasons – too little VBA and insufficient swing loft.

A key question is that, since VBA has not been broadly linked to performance, how have swings changed over time at the major league level to increase levels of VBA? In other words, where did the trend come from? While we don't know if the best hitters implemented this as a conscious or subconscious mechanic, what we do know with certainty is that they strayed from conventional views. Understanding the detailed process of exactly how this happened could possibly lead to other valuable findings. It is also possible there is a stubbornness characteristic in the psychological "make-up" that led to the best hitters going their own way which could be examined as a potential source of value. Since the trend towards increased VBA is likely still in progress, the logical question is: How far is it going to go? Certainly, there must be a limit to the maximum degree of VBA, and we will examine this further in an upcoming chapter.

CHAPTER 3.
HORIZONTAL BAT ANGLE

There may not be a more fundamental improvement opportunity than increasing VBA; however, Horizontal Bat Angle (HBA) also has a link to performance and, as will be discussed later, plays an important role in determining swing loft. The figure below illustrates HBA.

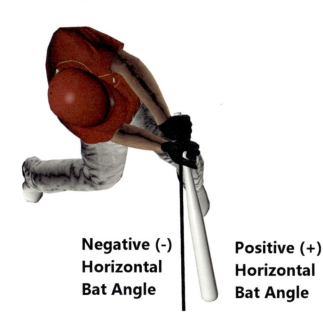

The degree of HBA in a particular swing is determined primarily by two factors: (1) The horizontal pitch location and (2) The player's pull or opposite field tendency. Another way to think about HBA is timing. Hitters tend to hit inside pitches early or more out in front (positive HBA) while they let outside pitches "travel" and get deeper in the zone (negative HBA).

Although most hitters have a slight pull-side bias, players who pull the ball excessively on middle pitches experience lower levels of consistency and performance than their peers. The angle of hit balls on middle pitches reveals the following relationship between hit direction and performance.

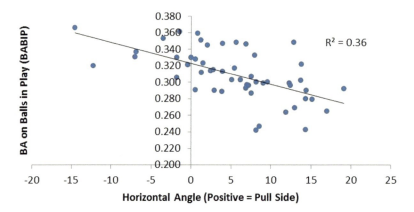

Chapter 3. Horizontal Bat Angle

For a particular hit, to move from simply assuming that HBA approximates the angle of a hit ball to calculating the actual HBA, the VBA must be known or estimated. This will be detailed in the next chapter. Here is why it matters. Take a bat and position it with zero VBA and approximately 20° of positive HBA at a hypothetical contact point. If you hit the ball square, it will go 20° to the left. Now, consider lower pitches where you increase VBA but keep the same 20° of HBA. You'll notice that as you increase VBA, there is a transfer of horizontal direction to vertical direction. To test this, keep the same HBA and increase VBA until the bat is straight up and down (yes, it is an unrealistic contact position but it's just to gain conceptual understanding). You'll notice that the 20° of horizontal direction (for a hypothetical ball coming off the bat) has been converted to 20° of vertical direction, or loft.

Although there is a clear relationship between horizontal angle and BABIP, the data indicates the presence of a power offset that needs to be considered. Players who pull the ball more have lower BABIPs but higher isolated power percentages (ISO), which translate to a higher wRC+. Consider the relationship between power and pull-side bias as in the chart following (based on middle horizontal pitches only).

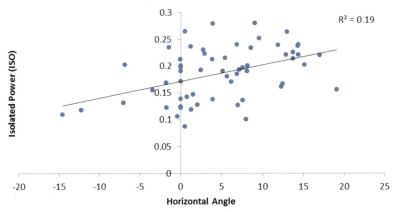

The key takeaway is that players with high levels of natural power have no need to sacrifice BABIP and consistency for power, which they already possess. In considering overall "quality of swing path", based on the data, there may be no player with a more effective path than Joey Votto. He is in the first quartile for all four key swing path metrics for every year since 2015 (one of only four players in the Qualified Player group): low spin, low standard deviation of launch angle, low IFFB rate, and low horizontal angle on middle pitches (1.2° to the pull side). There is no data on VBA; however, based on video samples and his extremely low IFFB rate, he is likely in the top quartile for VBA as well. The main point on HBA is this: Joey Votto has an average exit velocity on well-hit balls of 98.5 MPH, below the dataset average of 99.2 MPH, and yet he doesn't resort to pulling the ball to gain added power. For the 2015-2017 period, he was second only to Mike Trout in offensive production. I believe this makes a very strong case for anyone with aver-

Chapter 3. Horizontal Bat Angle

age or better power – quality of swing path trumps pull-side power gains.

The average horizontal hit angle by pitch location, based on the same Qualified Hitter dataset, is shown below. These values can be combined with the values of VBA by pitch location from the Fortenbaugh study to estimate average HBA angles for each pitch location, as shown in the table below.

	Vertical Bat Angle		
	Inside	Middle	Outside
High	24	22	21
Middle	32*	30	28*
Low	39	36	33

	Horizontal Hit Direction		
	Inside	Middle	Outside
High	14	3	-9
Middle	14	3	-7
Low	13	4	-5

$$HBA = \tan^{-1}\left[\sec\left(VBA \cdot \frac{\pi}{180}\right) \cdot \tan\left(Horizontal\ Angle \cdot \frac{\pi}{180}\right)\right] \cdot \frac{180}{\pi}$$

	Horizontal Bat Angle		
	Inside	Middle	Outside
High	15	3	-10
Middle	16	3	-8
Low	17	5	-6

The next chapter will detail the formulas for the above calculations. Two main conclusions can be drawn from the data on HBA: (1) Hitters are adjusting HBA based on horizontal pitch location and (2) Excessive pull-based power is not "free"; consequently, hitters with average or above average power are better served by focusing on improving swing path.

Chapter 4.
Swing Path – It's Not What You Think!

This is by far the most important chapter in this book, and I have written and re-written it several times. Here's the thing: If I miss the mark in my explanation, your ability to get maximum value from this book is at risk since a full understanding is required for effective implementation. What makes both the explanation and understanding so challenging is that it requires an understanding in 3D while we are both limited to a 2D format.

The quality of swing path is possibly second only to talent in determining success. It is also the area where consensus views appear the most misplaced. Since we know from the previous chapters that launch angle consistency is a characteristic of high-performing hitters, it is relatively safe to assume that improving bat loft consistency will improve ball loft consistency. Players have different power profiles, and therefore, will have different loft goals. However, once the goal has been established, consistent *total* bat loft in line with goal loft will improve overall performance.

If you examine current views on (ball) loft, you will notice two sources generally cited – the amount of loft coming from the path of the swing (also referred to as attack angle) and the contact point on the ball (i.e., above or below the ball equator). In general, swing loft is currently viewed as a one-dimensional factor as illustrated below.

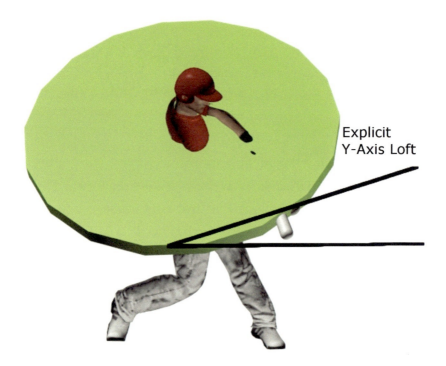

Swing path is indeed an aspect of bat loft – a very important one. As shown above, the plane around the hitter tilts from pitcher to catcher. To avoid terminology confusion, I'll call this Explicit Loft and associate it with the y-axis. The swing plane is formed by an x-y plane with Vertical Bat Angle (VBA) forming the x component. Horizontal Bat Angle (HBA), which can also be thought of as "timing", is placed on the z-axis.

Chapter 4. Swing Path – It's Not What You Think!

The Existence and Importance of Implicit Loft

Here is where things diverge from consensus views. Two additional factors influence bat loft but have never been publicly examined. Loft impact comes from both VBA and HBA, which also need to be considered in managing the total amount of bat loft at and around the contact point. Since the loft implications of VBA and HBA both depend on each other, these will be considered together as "Implicit Loft". Below are the fundamental "truths" of Implicit Loft based on what is physically observable. Referring to the previous illustrations of VBA and HBA or having a bat in hand may make these easier to understand:

The sign (+ or -) of Implicit Loft is dependent upon HBA (timing) while its magnitude depends upon the combination of both VBA and HBA.

- If HBA is positive (i.e., early, out in front contact for an inside pitch), Implicit Loft will be positive, provided VBA is positive (and it always should be).

- If HBA is negative (i.e., outside pitch, deeper in the zone contact), Implicit Loft will also be negative with magnitude determined by the combination of VBA and HBA, as described above.

The sensitivity of Implicit Loft is dependent upon VBA. As VBA increases, the sensitivity of Implicit Loft also increases. The directional influence of the sensitivity, however, depends upon whether HBA is positive or negative.

Consider the following illustration, in which all angles are the same with the exception of VBA.

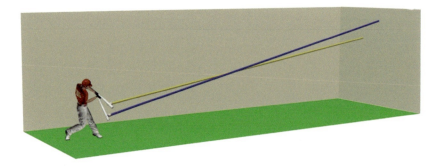

As is evident from the figure above, as VBA increases, horizontal direction is converted to vertical direction (i.e., the lower pitch in blue results in more loft and less direction to the left). This happens because HBA is positive as the ball is hit slightly out in front for an inside pitch. However, if HBA were negative for an outside pitch, the loft impact would be negative, with the new ball path lower and to the right of both the existing paths. Keep in mind that the focus here is still on *bat loft*; the ball's direction is being shown to illustrate what is happening to bat loft by examining ball path and assuming square (90°) contact.

Although hitters clearly get fooled on some pitches, data and video suggest that, the majority of the time, hitters are able to react to pitch location. Inside pitches are generally hit earlier or out in front while outside pitches are typically hit later or deeper in the zone. Different levels of VBA are also evident depending on pitch height, indicating that vertical adjustments are being made as well. Given the average VBA and HBA values for each pitch location, the amount of Implicit Loft can be calculated. In the table that follows,

Chapter 4. Swing Path – It's Not What You Think!

Explicit Loft (y-axis) is assumed to be zero. The formulas used to calculate the numbers in the tables are included at the end of the chapter.

	Total Implicit Loft		
	Inside	Middle	Outside
High	6.1	1.2	-3.4
Middle	8.6	1.7	-3.7
Low	10.3	2.9	-3.2

Given that these are derived from *average* values of VBA and HBA based on well-hit balls greater than 90 MPH, actual implicit bat loft differences are likely wider. The data may lead some to incorrectly conclude that loft on outside pitches is reconciled through a lower ball contact point (i.e., more backspin and loft); however, the data on the high-performing flat hitters indicates this is not the case – the loft adjustment being made is to Explicit Loft (y-axis).

Since Implicit Loft is a result of a hitter's reaction to pitch location, Implicit Loft dominates Explicit Loft. In other words, in order to reduce launch angle volatility as is evident in the swings of top performing hitters, players must adjust Explicit Loft so that the *total effective loft of the barrel at and around the contact point is consistent*. Another way to think about Implicit and Explicit Loft is that Implicit Loft comes from one point – ball contact and the compound bat angle at that point, whereas Explicit Loft comes from swing path. Thinking about Implicit Loft as "timing loft" may also be helpful; however, it is not technically correct since timing doesn't take VBA into consideration, a key component. It sounds like a very tall order – that the best hitters are (subconsciously) considering loft from an *expected* contact point and then adjusting Explicit Loft accordingly. However, the data suggests that these players are indeed making this adjustment. If you have doubts about a hitter's ability to make these complex adjustments in a very short time, there is a great book entitled *Blink* by Malcolm Gladwell that gives very convincing examples of the power of unconscious thinking. Shifting the focus from bat loft to ball loft, the existence of Implicit Loft is supported by the launch angle data by pitch location.

	Launch Angle by Pitch Location		
	Inside	Middle	Outside
All Balls	16.7	14.2	10.6
Well-Hit Balls >=90MPH	15.3	14.4	11.5
Backspin Hitting Group	12.3	11.0	8.2
Square Hitting Group	18.0	16.9	14.9

This is quite remarkable. The launch angle data given above confirms not only that Implicit Loft exists (i.e., difference between inside and outside pitches) but also that players are making adjustments to Explicit Loft to counterbalance Implicit Loft depending on the pitch location. In other words, the Implicit Loft differences between inside and outside pitches are even larger than the differences in the actual loft data. Also, notice how much larger launch angle is for the high-performing square hitting group than for the others. Their launch angles are not only meaningfully higher than those of both the average and the backspin hitting groups, but they also more actively adjust Explicit Loft, particularly on outside pitches. Given the differences

Chapter 4. Swing Path – It's Not What You Think!

that clearly come through in the data for the high-performing square hitting group:

1) The VBAs (x-values) are significantly higher.

2) The Explicit Loft (y-values) are much greater since their loft is not due to a lower ball contact point (i.e., backspin). Additionally, the lower ball loft volatility across the zone suggests greater Explicit Loft adjustments to counterbalance the effects of Implicit Loft.

3) The HBAs (z-values) are lower, indicating that they are not relying on a pull strategy to generate their above average loft.

Since the high-performing square hitters still show some difference between inside and outside launch angles, it is unknown whether completely closing the horizontal launch angle gap could improve performance even more. This is something that should be examined further.

The data suggests that the common instruction to hitters to "develop a consistent swing path" is a misnomer. In other words, a perfectly consistent path that does not account for Implicit Loft will result in *greater bat loft variability*! Thus, a more effective thought or instruction would be to *develop a consistent path for each pitch location*.

Optimal Loft Targets and Player Style

Optimal loft targets will, of course, vary slightly based on a particular player's average hit speed. Players with greater velocities benefit from higher loft targets. The chart below shows optimal run values based on the numerical factors used in the weighted on-base average (wOBA) formula (singles-.88, doubles-1.24, triples-1.59, home runs-2.05)

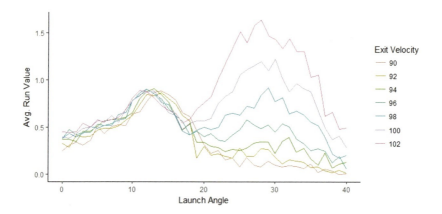

The chart above is based only on analyzing balls hit. However, similar to evaluating relative spin in the first chapter, examining ball performance alone is not relevant. What is important is player performance that includes variability – the full distribution of results. Due to variation in both launch angle and exit velocity, the chart looks significantly different once typical player distributions are considered.

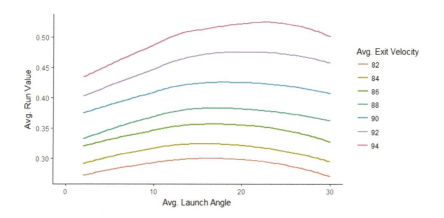

Chapter 4. Swing Path – It's Not What You Think!

Players with high average hit speeds will benefit from slightly greater launch angles. However, there is a "cost" side of the equation that needs to be considered. Strikeouts tend to increase as both exit velocity and launch angle increase, as depicted in the charts below. The following charts are based on the same Qualified Player group with averages based on reasonably well-hit balls (>=90MPH / LA >=0 <45) over the 2015-2017 period.

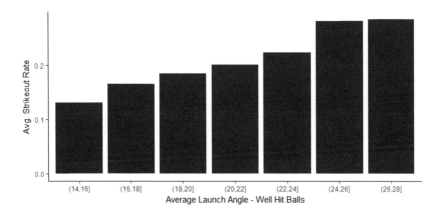

The chart squares with the reasoning that, as launch angle increases, the path of the bat is in the zone less. While some may prefer to examine contact rates as opposed to strikeouts, those metrics exhibit a very similar relationship as well. Players with higher average exit velocities on well-hit balls also experience a higher strikeout rate.

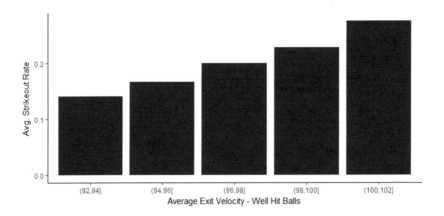

There is also a logical connection between mechanics and exit velocity. As players swing harder, they generally must commit earlier in their swings. Reviewing video makes evident that some players with high strikeouts have an earlier "point-of-no-return" in their swing.

I hope that the discussion and illustrations in this chapter were able to give you an understanding of what Implicit Loft is, why it matters, and how the best players are counterbalancing it with Explicit Loft to achieve high levels of performance. Given the ability to reasonably estimate bat loft for Implicit and Explicit Loft, it is relatively clear that the strikingly large difference in ball loft for the square hitting group is primarily the result of significantly greater Explicit Loft (y-axis).

Two other key takeaways are: (1) In addition to the square hitting group acquiring "knowledge" of VBA, they also seem to "know" more about the interaction between the loft factors based on the data. Given that this is likely subconscious knowledge, it points to the successful hitter's brain doing some amazing learning over the course of time

Chapter 4. Swing Path – It's Not What You Think!

and (2) Hitters performing below potential have a tremendous opportunity to identify and fix swing path problems with a high degree of certainty –we explore this in the next chapter.

Below details the formulas and math underlying the content of this chapter.

Quantitative Determination of Loft

Consider a coordinate system in which the x-y plane is parallel to the ground and the z-axis is normal to this plane, pointing upwards. The x-axis points from the catcher to the pitcher, and the y-axis is parallel to a line pointing from first base to third base. To account for Vertical Bat Angle (VBA), we first rotate by an angle ϕ about the x-axis. Similarly, to account for the (presently unknown) Horizontal Bat Angle (HBA), we rotate by an angle θ about the z-axis. The combination of these two rotations yields the following rotation matrix[6]:

$$\mathcal{R} = \begin{bmatrix} \cos\theta & -\sin\theta & 0 \\ \cos\phi\sin\theta & \cos\theta\cos\phi & -\sin\phi \\ \sin\theta\sin\phi & \cos\theta\sin\phi & \cos\phi \end{bmatrix}.$$

Assuming 90° or "square" contact as noted above, the ball's initial trajectory is characterized by the following vector:

$$\mathbf{r} = \mathcal{R} \cdot \begin{bmatrix} \cos t \\ \sin t \\ 0 \end{bmatrix}$$

and, as t→$\frac{\pi}{2}$, this simplifies to the following:

$$\mathbf{r} = \begin{bmatrix} \cos\theta \\ \sin\theta\cos\phi \\ \sin\theta\sin\phi \end{bmatrix},$$

up to a normalization factor.

Thus, HBA is given by

$$\theta(\alpha,\phi) = \tan^{-1}\left(\sec\phi \cdot \tan\alpha\right)$$

and the vertical hit direction, or Implicit Loft, is given by

$$\beta(\theta,\phi) = \arcsin\left[\frac{\sin\theta\sin\phi}{\sqrt{|\cos\theta|^2 + |\cos\phi\sin\theta|^2 + |\sin\theta\sin\phi|^2}}\right].$$

For each VBA ϕ, horizontal hit location α, and HBA θ previously presented in the chapter, the value of vertical hit direction β can be calculated and is provided in the Implicit Loft table above. Note that counter-clockwise is positive for both α and θ although α is measured from the x-axis while θ is measured from the negative y-axis.

Chapter 5.
Quantifying Optimal Swing Paths

Even though hitters should have different loft goals based on their exit velocities, the optimal mix of angles which form the swing path for each pitch location will be largely the same (except for small adjustments due to hitter bias or style).

There are two general approaches for players to implement the more effective swing path that is evident in the data. The first is for the player to simply change their thinking by removing the consensus-driven mechanic that is in conflict with the data. J. D. Martinez, possibly one of the most significant turnarounds in recent history, stated he was *thinking about swing path completely wrong* and had come to this realization after spending hours watching video of other players.

This chapter begins to detail the second method as the foundation for an extensive, precision-based training approach.

The best "information" for hitters is that which they can see and feel. Once the optimal combinations of x (VBA), y (Explicit Loft), and z (HBA) are known for each pitch location, visual summaries and training with the "solved" optimal swing path can help transfer the information directly to muscle memory. Consider the following illustration for two different pitch locations, which shows very different swing paths and angles for a hitter with a 15° loft goal.

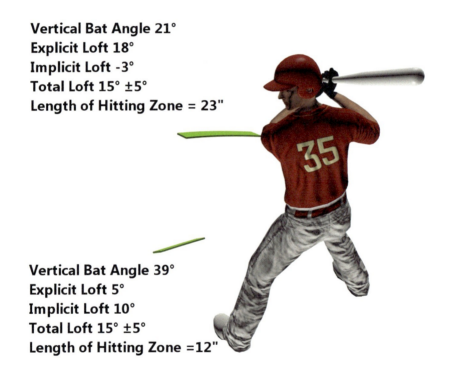

Vertical Bat Angle 21°
Explicit Loft 18°
Implicit Loft -3°
Total Loft 15° ±5°
Length of Hitting Zone = 23"

Vertical Bat Angle 39°
Explicit Loft 5°
Implicit Loft 10°
Total Loft 15° ±5°
Length of Hitting Zone =12"

As illustrated above, the total effective loft of the barrel at contact is 15° for both swings; however, the source of the bat loft is significantly different – primarily Explicit Loft for the high outside pitch while mainly Implicit Loft for the low inside pitch. To many hitters, the Implicit Loft that results

Chapter 5.   Quantifying Optimal Swing Paths

from an earlier contact point doesn't *feel* like loft. Devices and training methods to implement the specific mechanics of the visual above will be introduced later. Also, note the significantly shorter hitting zone for the lower pitch. We will also discuss and quantify this shortly.

One of the most encouraging revelations from the data is that many factors appear largely independent of talent. In other words, if the flat and backspin hitters showed little difference in loft levels, loft variability, and bat angles, it would suggest talent was the primary differentiator. Also consider that the significant differences in the metrics were for Qualified Players – professional hitters earning at least 502 plate appearances in each of the past three years. The differences between these two professional player groups imply even greater potential upside for hitters at lower levels of play.

Before we dive into the quantitative discussion, the message of the above to the intuitive-focused reader or player is that potential improvement can be realized by simply removing some of the consensus thoughts that are in opposition with the data such as "keep the bat level" or "hit with backspin". Substituting simple thoughts such as "increase swing loft on outside pitches" or "let the bat do the (loft) work on inside pitches" can go a long way and do not require an in-depth understanding of the quantification process to derive optimal angle combinations.

Any systematic solution for swing path must certainly allow for individual player style and consider hit ball speeds, pull or opposite field hitting tendencies, and VBA bias. Once the loft goal and the individual biases relating to path have been determined, the amount of Explicit Loft for each pitch location can be calculated as follows:

$$\text{Explicit Loft} = \text{Loft Goal} - \sin^{-1}\left[\sin\left(HBA \cdot HBA_{bias} \cdot \frac{\pi}{180}\right) \cdot \sin\left(VBA \cdot VBA_{bias} \cdot \frac{\pi}{180}\right)\right]$$

	Inside		Middle		Outside	
	Explicit	Implicit	Explicit	Implicit	Explicit	Implicit
High	8.9	6.1	13.8	1.2	18.4	-3.4
Middle	6.4	8.6	13.3	1.7	18.7	-3.7
Low	4.7	10.3	12.1	2.9	18.2	-3.2

Explicit Loft adjustments required to maintain consistent bat loft at contact are significant and range from 5°-19°, depending on pitch location. The total *bat loft* is the same – 15° for each pitch location. However, note the difference in where the loft is coming from for each of the different pitch locations.

For the majority of players, the swing for the low inside pitch location with only five degrees of Explicit Loft will *feel completely different* from the high outside pitch which requires 18° of Explicit Loft, even though the total effective bat loft is exactly the same for both pitch locations. Given that the high-performing flat hitting group had a three-degree spread between the loft on inside and outside pitches, hitters may desire to use model inputs consistent with these metrics.

The Hitting Zone – Smaller and More Variable Than You Might Think

Since the total effective amount of bat loft (explicit and implicit) can be measured at and around the contact point,

Chapter 5. Quantifying Optimal Swing Paths

we can provide a desired range of loft and calculate the actual length of the hitting zone for each pitch location. From an intuitive perspective, if you position a bat so as to increase VBA to straight up and down (granted, this is an unrealistic angle), you can see how the loft of the barrel changes rapidly. In other words, in this position, only one point will loft the ball at a particular launch angle. Moving the bat to the other extreme – completely horizontal, significantly increases the potential to loft the ball at a particular angle. The length of the hitting zone can be measured mathematically (see a detailed explanation at the end of the chapter) for each pitch location and results in the following:

	Size of Hitting Zone (Inches)		
	Inside	Middle	Outside
High	20	22	23
Middle	15	16	17
Low	12	14	15

Since increased levels of VBA produce flatter contact, less launch angle variability, and improved performance, this suggests improving the bat's "time in the zone" by utilizing less VBA would not be an effective strategy. In other words, increased levels of VBA trump "time in the zone". This differs considerably from the current consensus belief.

The size of the hitting zone for each pitch location was calculated based on the values of VBA and HBA presented in Chapter 3 as follows:

The Explicit Loft Ψ to produce a loft goal of γ is given by

$\Psi = \gamma - \sin^{-1}(\sin\theta \sin\phi)$.

Since total launch angle variability could be described in terms of its components of bat loft variability and ball loft variability, then, provided sufficient data, separate training goals for these two components could be established. The example below assumes a player with a 15° loft goal with a target variance of ±5° coming from bat loft variability. The length of the arc s that would produce loft within the desired range is given by

$$s = R\Delta\theta$$

where R is the radius of the approximate distance to the barrel contact point and is the change in HBA as it travels along the arc. The radius of the arc through the contact point is assumed constant and was estimated by the author; however, this metric could be a custom input based on player-specific data.

Manipulating the first equation above yields

$$\theta = \sin^{-1}\left[\frac{\sin(\gamma - \psi)}{\sin(\phi)}\right]$$
$$= \sin^{-1}\left[\frac{\sin(\beta)}{\sin(\phi)}\right].$$

Thus,

$$\Delta\theta = \sin^{-1}\left[\frac{\sin(\beta + \delta\gamma)}{\sin(\phi)}\right] - \sin^{-1}\left[\frac{\sin(\beta - \delta\gamma)}{\sin(\phi)}\right].$$

Chapter 5. Quantifying Optimal Swing Paths

If it is assumed that the amount of Explicit Loft is constant throughout the path on the arc, then the lengths of the arcs that will produce hits within the acceptable range of lofts for each pitch location are given in the Size of Hitting Zone (Inches) table above.

Interestingly, the length of the hitting zone varies significantly based on the location of the pitch and the resulting levels of VBA and HBA. A visual summary representing the optimal angle combinations, the target Explicit Loft, and the size of the hitting zone is provided towards the beginning of the chapter, which may be more user-friendly than the quantitative explanation given above. Although the two paths in the illustration have very different angle combinations and are visually very different, both sets of angles result in the same 15° of loft, assuming square contact.

Chapter 6.

Putting It All Together:

The Swing Path and Angles That Make Joey Votto Different

Over the 2015-2017 seasons, Joey Votto was the second-best hitter in baseball – next to the super-human Mike Trout. In analyzing the previously discussed metrics that contribute to contact quality – low spin, low standard deviation of launch angle, and low IFFB rate, Joey Votto is one of only four players in the top quartile for each period. For the very important VBA, no data has been consistently collected for all players; however, his difference in that area is striking based on video sampling. Joey Votto is famous in the Sabermetric community for hardly ever hitting an infield fly ball. Interestingly, the reason why can be seen in his different angles.

		Vertical Bat Angle			Horizontal Bat Angle		
		Inside	Middle	Outside	Inside	Middle	Outside
High	Votto	35	34	33	21	-3	-10
	Average	24	22	21	15	3	-10
	Diff	11	12	12	6	-6	0
Middle	Votto	45	37	35	19	4	-6
	Average	32	30	28	16	3	-8
	Diff	13	7	7	3	1	2
Low	Votto	48	39	37	23	6	-1
	Average	39	36	33	17	5	-6
	Diff	9	3	4	6	1	5

As the data makes clear, his performance is different because his angles are different. Consider Votto's VBA and HBA relative to average (the step that converts horizontal hit angle to HBA is identical to that described in the previous chapter and has been omitted). Similar to calculating Implicit Loft based on overall averages for VBA and HBA, we can do the same for Joey Votto. Based on his angles, his Implicit Loft values by pitch location are as follows:

		J. Votto - Implicit Loft		
		Inside	Middle	Outside
High	Votto	12	-2	-6
	Average	6	1	-3
	Diff	6	-3	-2
Middle	Votto	13	2	-3
	Average	9	2	-4
	Diff	5	0	0
Low	Votto	17	4	-1
	Average	10	3	-3
	Diff	6	1	3

Let's switch from considering bat loft to ball loft; here are Votto's launch angles on well-hit balls by pitch location:

Chapter 6. Putting It All Together

	Launch Angle - Well Hit Balls		
	Inside	Middle	Outside
Joey Votto	19.0	18.8	16.8
Low-Backspin Group	18.0	16.9	14.9
Average	15.3	14.4	11.5

Take a moment and see if you can identify how Votto's bat angles and sources of bat loft differ from the averages. Can you see what might be driving his solid contact and extremely low IFFB rate?

Joey Votto has significantly higher VBA levels across the board. On high inside pitches, he is also considerably different with respect to HBA, contacting those pitches much earlier (out in front) than the average player. The high inside pitch location is where the most IFFBs come from. It is likely no coincidence that his greatest Implicit Loft difference relative to average is the high inside pitch location. Another major difference is where he is getting his (ball) loft on the middle and outside pitches – his Explicit Loft (y-axis).

Since the data as well as the observed physical characteristics link VBA to quality contact and higher performance, it's no surprise that Votto exhibits very high levels of VBA. Given all of Votto's metrics that have been previously considered, there is a strong possibility that he has the best swing path and angles of any current hitter in major league baseball. There is no questioning the talent of a player like Mike Trout, who has better overall performance; however, Votto is hitting the ball flatter (less spin), with lower launch angle volatility, and lower IFFB rate – all indicating he has a better swing path than Mike Trout. Trout has a 3.5 MPH exit velocity advantage which likely accounts for most of the difference in their wRC+ (three-year average of 173 for Trout vs. 166 for Votto). Recall that Votto is generating his performance with average exit velocity. It's interesting to consider that Mike Trout could possibly be even better than he currently is if he had Votto's swing path and angles – that is a scary thought!

What is so encouraging for struggling or underperforming hitters is that optimal angles can be quantified and visually represented for hitters to see and feel so that anyone can have a swing path and angles similar to those of Joey Votto. This is explored in the next chapter.

Chapter 7.
Implementation and Training Methods

Also interesting to consider is how the group of top-performing square hitters acquired their swing paths that distinctly differ from everyone else. Certainly, the odds of them getting ideas from analyzing spin data or doing linear algebra to determine optimal mixes of Implicit versus Explicit Loft are very low. It suggests, however, that there is likely a highly effective, iterative training process that allowed subconscious learning at a very high level. Since the data indicates that players are adjusting Explicit Swing Loft based on pitch location to counterbalance Implicit Loft, some very impressive things are happening in the hitter's brain. It also implies that players who have bought into such consensus views as "hit with backspin" or "level bat" have put in place hard-wired "overrides" that are likely having a negative impact on performance.

In all of the baseball instruction I've ever witnessed, I've never heard anyone instruct a player to hit with more Vertical

Bat Angle (VBA), and yet both video and data suggest this is required for more consistent square contact and significantly improved performance. Since many in the consensus believe high levels of VBA are a primary *cause* of weakly hit balls and pop-ups, it will likely be a very long time before that view changes by a full 180° to align with the data.

Various ways exist to implement the optimal paths and angles being used by the best hitters and discussed previously. Listed below are two possibilities – a high-level, visual approach and a detailed, high-precision method.

High-Level (Visual) Method

I believe many hitters will be surprised to discover that once they eliminate the incorrect thinking, the brain will allow things to move in the correct direction with a typical iterative training process. Since the brain seems to speak a visual language when it comes to sports motions, having an idea of what the angles look like for the different pitch locations will be helpful. Therefore, images for two pitch locations have been added at the end of this section.

Before making any changes, it is important to know your starting point. In other words, hit balls off practice pitching and note the variability of the launch angles – that tells you the current quality of your path and angles. Any measurement with video in terms of VBA or calculating the variability of launch angles will likely be helpful.

I believe the subconscious brain's favorite teacher is the ball – probably because it doesn't talk! By simply hitting

Chapter 7. Implementation and Training Methods   65

pitched balls and observing launch angle variability, things should move in a positive direction. This iterative training process of keeping what works (in reducing variability) and discarding what doesn't is likely how the best hitters came to "know" everything previously discussed.

After doing the above process with middle pitches, do the same with different pitch locations, noting the variability of launch angles with each location. An additional factor that players can observe is spin. Is the ball coming off the bat relatively flat or with significant backspin? Too much backspin indicates that the bat may be too flat (i.e., VBA is too low) or that there is not enough Explicit Loft. This method may take a little longer than the detailed method below, but many will find it more fun, a key factor particularly for younger players. However, if for some reason the launch angle variability is higher than desired or fails to narrow, the precision method described below may help.

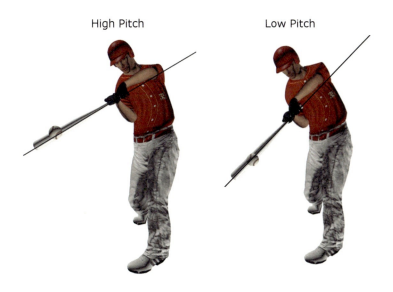

Notice how the plane extends through the upper chest area regardless of the pitch location. If, on the other hand, the plane extends through the mid-section of the body, VBA is likely insufficient. At each pitch location, the plane should start at the ball and then extend through the handle of the bat into the upper body Take a moment to visualize different pitch locations and what these planes might look like.

High-Precision Methods

An advantage of a high-precision, detailed method is that changes in total bat loft can be very difficult to feel, particularly when dealing with Implicit Loft that just "seems to happen". Once a player has determined the target loft goal, the optimal mix of angle combinations can be calculated for each pitch location. A device that I developed has its upper assembly mounted on a ball joint so that it can adjust to any desired combination of angles for VBA (x-axis), Explicit Swing Loft (y-axis), and HBA (z-axis).

Chapter 7. Implementation and Training Methods 67

Optimal angles for each pitch location can be summarily represented through an angle guide custom made for each player or an iPhone app (in development) which uses the device's gyroscope to set the angle combinations. Additional information can be found at www.hittingtech.com.

By using the above or a similar method for static training, users can see and feel the optimal angle combinations. Players should then add pitched balls for dynamic training. The general method is the same as described in the visual method; only players can use more precision by analyzing VBA from video as well as obtaining actual standard deviation of launch angles based on ball flight. My experience with upper-level players with good swing paths is that a standard deviation of 12-14 degrees off practice pitching is achievable. Hitters should alternate between static and dynamic training methods to reduce launch angle volatility for each pitch location.

Player Interviews

Both data and video can be utilized to identify players who are using incorrect "thinking". Players don't always do what they think, and so it is difficult to tell whether their incorrect "thinking" is in the conscious or subconscious. I believe the majority of players fall into the first category – they have some conscious "override" which is getting in the way. J. D. Martinez is an example of the first type – he was consciously thinking about the swing completely wrong. Player interviews can go a long way in determining which players are consciously thinking about swing path and bat angles in a way that is inconsistent with data-proven mechanics.

Effective Until Proven Otherwise

There have likely been many players who have allowed some of the effective, non-consensus mechanics to creep into their swings but were corrected to the "right method" somewhere along the line. Although considerable mystery surrounds how the subconscious brain learns at high levels,

I believe the industry would do well to trust that process a little more and validate key mechanical advice with data or video before recommending implementation. Think about it from this perspective: What do you think the first player who ever tried VBA was told? It turns out, whoever it was, that their subconscious "knowledge" was correct. More importantly, the value of their discovery is still not being considered by the baseball "establishment".

Training Devices

Many popular training devices discourage the effective swing path mechanics that have been discussed. The traditional baseball tee, for example, discourages increased levels of VBA due to greater contact with the tee stem as bat angle steepens. Many other devices advocate the same path regardless of ball location. With an enlightened view based on previously presented data, any device can now be effectively evaluated to determine if it is consistent with the swing path and angles of the high-performing flat hitting group. At a minimum, devices should facilitate high levels of VBA and allow for changes in VBA, Explicit Loft, and HBA dependent on pitch location.

Chapter 8.
A Story of Unlikely Discovery

My general interest in examining opportunity relative to consensus views comes from my experience as a research analyst and member of an investment team. The specific idea of looking at potential opportunities in baseball started in 2007 … at a tennis tournament with my son, who was just getting started with baseball. We were watching Andy Roddick, who was being coached by Jimmy Connors, warm up for a match. They got into an argument about how to hit a mid-court forehand. Connors wanted him to step across with his left foot, and Roddick made a tripping motion as if to say, "I can't hit it that way". I was shocked. By 2007, the "new" forehand had completely transformed the game, and its effectiveness was beyond any doubt. However, many in the tennis "establishment" rejected the change, favoring the "old way" instead. How could they possibly believe this? There was simply no basis or justification. In seeking out pros to learn more about the new forehand and teach me the specific mechanics, it was very common to hear, "You don't want to learn that because it's not really better". This experience was the basis for my questioning hitting mechanics going into baseball. What old or ineffective mechanics might the baseball establishment be holding onto? From my experience with tennis, I believed the answer could be found by examining what the best hitters were doing.

At the time, I was playing golf periodically and was fascinated with the complexity of the mechanics. I was never a good golfer but came to appreciate the importance of the swing path, which seemed to be a primary driver of success. I found a large metal circular swing plane at a driving range, and using it seemed to improve my swing path and results. This device would be very instrumental and come into play later, as one of my first product attempts was an aluminum swing path ring for hitting. Conceptually, the idea was good, but its size and implementation rendered it a complete failure.

By 2012, I was spending a considerable amount of time analyzing professional swings and trying to find specifics that set them apart. I had developed a device based on a ball joint in which compound angles allowed an x-y plane to be adjusted for a hitter to see and feel an effective swing path. I created a list of players with very poor paths that I believed could be systematically improved. At the top of the list was J. D. Martinez. In early 2012, I sent a letter and video to his team, presenting an idea for systematic improvement for players in general, using his case specifically given his extremely poor swing path. I never heard back. In the latter part of 2013, he had radically changed his swing, and in December there was an article on Fangraphs entitled *Rule*

Chapter 8. A Story of Unlikely Discovery

5 Darkhorse J.D. Martinez to which I made these comments (my name on the site was Swingdoc):

> "These changes are some of the most significant (and in the right direction!) that I have seen for a major league player.... if he keeps moving his swing in this direction, he will be a major offensive producer in the next few seasons."

He unsuccessfully pleaded with his team to keep him based on his swing changes, and they released him just a few months later. He would indeed go on to become one of the best hitters in baseball in one of the most significant turnarounds in the modern game. Credit and thanks to Dan Farnsworth for writing the article.

This story and other similar ones led me to believe two things. First, the research I had been doing seemed to be very much on the right track. Second, when I put everything together – the absurdity of key findings coming from other sports, the research process in my profession, and cases of truly unbelievable accuracy and timing in projecting players – it was quite clear to me that it was all due to divine inspiration and timing.

From my vantage point, I saw many other J. D. Martinez-type opportunities in professional baseball and thought there would be interest in at least looking into other potential cases with similar issues. I contacted teams, agents, players, and a host of indirect contacts. I struck out at every turn.

For the next couple of years, I sidelined the idea of convincing anyone else of my findings and refocused my efforts on product development based on the same research.

I learned some programming with the hope of adding technology-based functionality to my existing product as well as exploring several other product possibilities. It was very challenging but at the same time rewarding. I'm still a bad programmer, but I can now program poorly in different languages!

In the summer of 2016, I came across another player who had recently been called up and was projected to do very well. I noticed that he had made a very recent swing change that would make success virtually impossible at the major league level. I made the following comment to the article "Scouting Astros Call Up Alex Bregman" written by Eric Longenhagen:

"Only the power and HRs won't be there consistently because he is cutting his swing so short. With his current approach, I think he's going to have a far tougher road than what most people are expecting"

His issue was a very common flaw that I had come across in my research as well as working with hitters. Players were getting fooled by looking at video or pictures and seeing a short or bent front arm of professional hitters. These players had then mistakenly adopted a secondary, last-resort adjustment made on inside pitches – shortening the front arm during the swing and building that into their primary mechanics. Bregman's initial performance was exactly what I had expected – little to no power and a horrendous start going 2 for 38.

On August 7th, I noticed he had changed his swing and had also made comments in the media regarding the swing

Chapter 8. A Story of Unlikely Discovery

change. Upon reviewing video of his most recent game, I noticed he had indeed discovered and fixed the problem. I made an updated comment to the same article.

"...since his terrible start and now likely subsequent improvement may be cast as randomness, better luck, or just needing more major league ABs, I think the real story here is relatively clear – the changes in his mechanics and approach were the primary driving factors both on the way down and the way back up (hopefully?) and would have occurred regardless of the playing level (AAA or MLB)".

Bregman did go on to turn things around in dramatic fashion, and he has performed well ever since. He later changed his story – stating that he didn't make a swing change – but this obviously contradicts his initial statements as well as what is factually observable from video. I can only speculate that this change in his public statements was so that nobody got "thrown under the bus".

Over the years, I have made less than 20 player projections – all on the same site. I missed on a couple but the accuracy and timing on most led me to believe that I was indeed onto something of value. I never projected any player (other than J. D. Martinez) to transform from well below average to a top MLB hitter, and I also never "flipped" any projection other than that of Alex Bregman. I'm not sure of the exact odds of projecting a significant turnaround with the timing correct to within three at bats, but I'm sure they are very long. Combining these timely projections with the highly unlikely path of discovery deepened my belief that God was using all of it for a greater purpose.

In late-2016, with almost two years of Statcast data available, I began to explore whether my video findings could be proven quantitatively. The low-spin square hitting question was my first project. The alignment of the data with the video research was considerable – all the key metrics of path quality aligned. In mid-2017 with a more solid foundation based on the data, I again attempted to see if there was interest. Certainly, with the J. D. Martinez and Alex Bregman projections to reference, combined with an initial attempt to quantify swing path, I thought the case for general consideration was reasonably good. I don't know the total number of contacts that I attempted but it was likely in the hundreds. One thing really stuck out – in almost every case, people *concluded before they considered*. It simply didn't make logical sense because the downside was extremely limited. I tried to emphasize the overall risk-reward profile: "What's the downside of a player who is close to crashing out of baseball anyway?" I did get one phone meeting with a major league organization that pushed the conversation to the organization's player development side. They really had no interest in anything on the data side. I felt like I had one arm tied behind my back as they wanted to keep things "old school". The conversations ended up going nowhere.

As with my previous attempts, I went back to work on the device side. Just as everything was close to launch, I talked to some resellers and realized that potential buyers would have no idea of how or why training for optimal angle combinations could significantly improve swing path and performance. *A different swing path for each pitch location?*

Chapter 8. A Story of Unlikely Discovery

– *That's crazy!* A complete re-education of the market would be required.

I looked at the list of strategic alternatives that I had compiled at the outset. The list was ranked based on potential economic return. The last item was "Write a Book". I really didn't *want* to write a book. If I couldn't get anyone to consider the findings before, how would a book change that? Then something dawned on me. What if God's purpose in all this was simply to glorify Him? The book might have been *my* last choice, but perhaps this was the route that glorified Him the most. As a Christian, the area in which I have fallen woefully short is in my witness to others. With all the paths leading in this direction, it seems that fixing my witness deficiency may have been part of the plan. I came to believe early on that everything I had come to understand was a result of divine inspiration. Ideas from completely unrelated areas, and yet in hindsight, I had to go down those paths in order to find them. At other times, ideas came completely out of nowhere, once after I had totally given up on everything and decided to go in a different direction. Looking back, all the road blocks look very different from the opposite side – they all have arrows pointing in the direction that led things here.

Chapter 9.
Key Bat and Body Adjustments

You may now be thinking, "Swing path may be important, but it certainly can't be *everything*". In this section, I will highlight some key findings from my video research that is not currently quantifiable with publicly available data.

Swing path is indeed not the only thing; however, in many cases, the body will correctly align with swing path so that the two work together. There are a few common body-related issues that can get in the way, and I will discuss those shortly. Generally speaking, the axis of the upper spine will be broadly consistent with the axis created by the *x-y* (or VBA-Explicit Loft) plane as in the following illustration.

The most common problem with swing plane and body position not matching is that, in order for a hitter to feel the correct path, both palms must be working on the path with left/right palms opposing. In many cases, hitters will get the top hand too counter-clockwise rotated (for a right-handed hitter), making feeling the correct path difficult. As a result, to get the bat on plane, excessive side bend is needed to make everything work. While side bend is correctly used as an adjustment for low pitches, considerable side bend for every pitch location because of over-rotation of the top palm is problematic. To be more specific, it is not really "palm up/palm down" as is commonly referenced but rather that the opposing palms must be "on-plane" with the swing path. I have noticed a few MLB players who are naturally right handed and swing left that seem to have a particular issue with this problem. I'm not sure of the exact reason but I

Chapter 9. Key Bat and Body Adjustments

think the non-dominant hand may be harder to feel as being "on-plane".

Adjustments Are in One Direction Only

There is simply not enough time in hitting to adjust in two directions. Just as hitters operate in one-decision mode for the swing (i.e., the default is always to swing with a one-sided decision to stop the swing), the same is evident in other areas where hitters need to make adjustments. The angle of the bat, for example, only moves in a flattening adjustment direction in reaction to higher pitches. This can be easily verified by trying to hit a low pitch starting with a very flat bat position. You will notice this feels unnatural and awkward. Conversely, start with a steeper bat position at launch and then adjust flatter for a higher pitch. You will notice that this feels much more natural.

Interestingly, the body works in the exact opposite direction. The body only adjusts in a lower direction through three factors – a slight "sitting into the swing", very minor adjustments in the lower spine angle (increase), and increased side bend that steepens the bat angle. If you start with any of these three in the "low" pitch-location extreme, you will notice it is much more difficult to straighten up for pitches higher in the zone.

A Common Pre-Launch Movement

From the video analysis, I identified one particular pre-launch movement that many of the great hitters seemed to have in common. It is a square-to-steep-to-square bat sequence. In other words, the hitter started out with the bat square to his spine angle. Just as the pitch is released, the bat angle goes steep, and then the bat flattens as much as is necessary for the location of the pitch being hit. During this last sequence, as the bat is flattening to get "on-plane", it finds alignment with the body, which is adjusting in the opposite direction. The majority of these adjustments are made prior to the "point of no return" – after that, very few, if any adjustments are possible.

In working with hitters, it seemed that the "square-to-spine" start somehow gave an image to the hitter's brain in terms of the bat-body plane matching that occurs later in the swing, as each approaches the "matching point" from opposite directions.

Chapter 10.
Final Thoughts

In the 2008 financial crisis, there was one consensus view at the heart of the problem. It was the belief that, because housing prices had never gone down nationally on a sustained basis that they wouldn't do so in the future. When markets get to the point where most participants believe the same projection, they are almost certain to go in the opposite direction. A few investors made billions by betting against the consensus. The current views in baseball appear similar. I haven't conducted a poll; however, based on my experience, I would guess that the majority of people in baseball don't believe there is a competitive advantage to be gained relative to hitting mechanics, especially by connecting them to data. Just like the housing issue, the expectation is based on past history – it has never been done before.

In investment research, if you decide not to own a company in the benchmark that you are being measured against (like the S&P 500), you are making an implicit "bet" against that company. It is largely the same in the case with baseball. Now that you've read and considered the findings, it is constructive to know what you need to believe to take the other side of the argument. Either you have to believe that the best hitters are going in the wrong direction with increased levels of VBA and the square contact that goes along with it, OR you have to believe that hitters can't easily change their path and angles. In regard to the first issue, proof of hitters increasing VBA is easily seen from historical video. Given that, it seems a sizable bet that somehow, this time, the amazing athletic brain and the typical improvement process in all sports are somehow absent. This is a *very* large bet. In regard to the second issue – the ability of any underperforming hitter to implement the findings, the bet is smaller simply because it hasn't been broadly proven. Of course, once it has, the opportunity for competitive advantage will be lost. Thus, the second issue should be further considered from a risk-reward perspective. Given the significant performance difference in the data as well as select cases like J. D. Martinez, who simply *changed their thinking* to move away from consensus views, the potential upside is considerable. The risk side of the equation is very player specific. Because, as previously discussed, the quality of path can be assessed relatively quickly, players should be able to test the impact of any contemplated change before making a firm commitment. For players underperforming their desired level, the downside is limited. The main point is that, whatever your view, there is no logical basis for a summary rejection without at least some examination and consideration.

The evidence strongly suggests that multitudes of players at all levels are underperforming their full potential primarily because of wrong thinking about swing path. Since the complexity of swing path can be quantified, solved, simplified, and visually represented for players to see and feel optimal paths for each pitch location, the "cure" rate for poor swing paths should be very high. Given the slow uptake rate on new ideas in baseball, there is likely a sustainable competitive advantage to be had by implementing the findings previously discussed.

Only God knows the size and scope of the new findings. If I had to bet on high probability outcomes that will come to pass within the next 20 years, they would be as follows: (1) Underperformance due to wrong thinking simply won't exist. With the knowledge, tools, and technology now available, it is simply too easy to fix. Sure, the bar is always changing, as the best hitters continually move mechanics in a positive direction; however, the gap between the two will likely shrink considerably. (2) Either the research process or the organizational structure at the highest levels of baseball where these things are considered will change in some meaningful way. Although there is no market mechanism (relative to investment analysis) that forces reconciling views on a regular basis, this type of "idea accountability" is too easily added and too valuable to not be part of a solid research process. Asking the question of where you might be wrong or what you might be missing is extremely difficult. Even knowing the value and doing it for years in my profession, it is something I have to force myself to do every day. (3) The "gap in the middle" between the research and player development sides of organizations will close. The challenge is that there is no career path, and consequently, no available talent pool, that encompasses experience on both sides – data analysis and mechanics. It is clear, however, that value will not be maximized without those two sides *thinking together*. The merging of mechanics and data is a key underpinning for everything in this book. While I had some professional training on one side, I had to teach myself the other and benefited from starting with a "clean slate".

The opportunity at the lower levels of baseball for players and parents may be the largest. It is unlikely things will change significantly in these groups any time soon as change resulting from the trickle-down process is likely far into the future. While this will create tremendous opportunities, it is also fraught with challenges as players with different views (and swings) will experience friction from the "systems" in which they play.

As stated at the beginning of this book, I don't take for granted that the data will change your views on hitting. However, I will share one last, very convincing piece of information. On baseballsavant.com, video for hitters is available and can be filtered for certain pitch locations. Go to "Statcast Search" and select "Batter". In "Gameday Zones", enter 3 and 12 – those are up and in pitch locations for a left-handed hitter. Input "Votto, Joey" for "Batters". Select "Only Show Plays with Video". Select a result and pause the video at contact. You will notice a very high level of VBA. This is why Joey Votto hardly ever hits a "pop-up" – it is almost physically impossible given his level of VBA.

Chapter 10. Final Thoughts

Until you start hearing "Hey, little Zack, your bat is *way too flat! more bat angle!, more bat angle! and add more swing loft on the outside pitch!*" at local practice facilities, a meaningful competitive advantage will exist for all who are willing to consider what has been presented. Just as progress in other fields cannot be deterred, accurate synthesis of the data will continue to challenge and change thinking to align with reality. Given that the Statcast data has been available just a few short years, it is possible that the opportunity for an advantage will never be larger.

As I look back to the path that led me to write this book, I often think – "Wow, what are the odds?" Some of the events are extremely low probability by themselves but when everything in the chain that had to happen is combined, it is a level of possibility that I cannot fathom. Even more, the failure and disappointment at multiple turns over the past several years was *required* for everything to come together. Early on, I knew God's hand was at work, but I had no idea the journey would lead here. The journey has deepened my faith and made me realize the purpose of it all – To God be the Glory!

Endnotes

1   Statista, "Number of participants in baseball in the United States from 2006 to 2016 (in millions)" statista.com. **https://www.statista.com/statistics/191626/participants-in-baseball-in-the-us-since-2006/**

2   Data sources: *Baseball Savant, Fangraphs.* Accessed December 2017.

3   Alan M. Nathan (2017), "Analysis of Baseball Trajectories", http://baseball.physics.illinois.edu/TrajectoryAnalysis.pdf

4   Ted Williams with John Underwood (1971), *The Science of Hitting* (New York, NY: Simon & Schuster)

5   David Fortenbaugh (2011), "The Biomechanics of the Baseball Swing."

6   Mathematical equations developed specifically for this research by K.L. Utt, Physics PhD candidate, Washington University in St. Louis.

Glossary

Average Run Value – A custom calculated composite value utilizing the weights for singles, doubles, triples, and home runs based on the weights in the Weighted On-Base Percentage formula (see below)

Batting Average on Balls in Play (BABIP) – Measures how often a ball in play goes for a hit. A ball is "in play" when the plate appearance ends in something other than a strikeout, walk, hit batter, catcher's interference, sacrifice bunt, or home run. In other words, the batter put the ball in play and it didn't clear the outfield fence. Typically around 30% of all balls in play fall for hits, but there are several variables that can affect BABIP rates for individual players, such as defense, luck, and talent level. The formula for BABIP is as follows:

$BABIP = (H - HR)/(AB - K - HR + SF)$

Isolated Power (ISO) – Measures a hitter's raw power and tells you how often a player hits for extra bases. We know that not all hits are created equally and ISO provides you with a quick tool for determining the degree to which a given hitter provides extra base hits as opposed to singles.

While batting average and slugging percentage each offer part of the answer, they aren't very good at distinguishing players without being considered together, even if you know a player's walk rate as well.

For example, a four singles and zero home runs in 10 at bats is a .400 batting average and .400 slugging percentage. One home run and zero singles in 10 at bats is a .100 batting average and a .400 slugging percentage. The first player's ISO is .000 and the second player's ISO is .300, which tells you that the second player hits for extra bases more often. ISO doesn't replace a metric like OPS or wOBA, it simply helps you determine the type of player at which you're looking. ISO is calculated as follows (three different methods):

ISO = SLG – AVG

ISO = ((2B) + (2*3B) + (3*HR)) / AB

ISO = Extra Bases / At-Bats

ISO is not park or league adjusted, so you should treat it like batting average, on-base percentage, or slugging percentage when making comparisons. However, this makes it easy to calculate for small or large samples of data because the formula never changes.

Weighted On-Base Percentage (wOBA) – One of the most important and popular catch-all offensive statistics. It was created by Tom Tango to measure a hitter's overall offensive value, based on the relative values of each distinct offensive event. wOBA is based on a simple concept: Not all hits are created equal. Batting average assumes that they are.

Chapter 10. Glossary

On-base percentage does too, but does one better by including other ways of reaching base such as walking or being hit by a pitch.

The wOBA formula for the 2013 season was:

wOBA = (0.690×uBB + 0.722×HBP + 0.888×1B + 1.271×2B + 1.616×3B + 2.101×HR) / (AB + BB – IBB + SF + HBP)

These weights change on a yearly basis, so you can find the specific wOBA weights for every year from 1871 to the present here:: https://www.fangraphs.com/guts.aspx?type=cn

Weighted Runs Created (wRC) – An improved version of Bill James' Runs Created (RC) statistic, which attempted to quantify a player's total offensive value and measure it by runs. In Runs Created, instead of looking at a player's line and listing out all the details (e.g., 23 2B, 15 HR, 55 BB, 110 K, 19 SB, 5 CS), the information is synthesized into one metric in order to say, "Player X was worth 24 runs to his team last year". While the idea was sound, James' formula has since been superseded by Tom Tango's wRC, which is based off Weighted On-Base Average (wOBA)

Weighted Runs Created Plus (wRC+) – Measures how a player's wRC compares with league average after controlling for park effects. League average for position players is 100, and every point above 100 is a percentage point above league average. For example, a 125 wRC+ means a player created 25% more runs than a league average hitter would have in the same number of plate appearances. Similarly, every point below 100 is a percentage point below league average, so a 80 wRC+ means a player created 20% fewer runs than league average. wRC+ is park and league-adjusted, allowing one to to compare players who played in different years, parks, and leagues. Want to know how Ted Williams compares with Albert Pujols in terms of offensive abilities? This is your statistic. wRC+ is the most comprehensive rate statistic used to measure hitting performance because it takes into account the varying weights of each offensive action and then adjusts them for the park and league context in which they took place. The formula for wRC is:

wRC = (((wOBA-League wOBA)/wOBA Scale)+(League R/PA))*PA.

Additional information on Glossary terms can be found at Fangraphs.com

Made in United States
Troutdale, OR
09/12/2023

12849516R00057